# Patrick Stewart

Sir Patrick Stewart is a renowned British actor, born on July 13, 1940, in Mirfield, West Yorkshire, England. He is best known for his iconic role as Captain Jean-Luc Picard in the television series "Star Trek: The Next Generation" (1987-1994) and in subsequent Star Trek films. Stewart's portrayal of the thoughtful and diplomatic captain garnered him widespread acclaim and a dedicated fan following.

Before his breakthrough role in "Star Trek," Patrick Stewart had an extensive career in theater. He was a member of the Royal Shakespeare Company (RSC) and performed in various Shakespearean plays, including memorable performances as Macbeth and Prospero. His stage work earned him critical praise and established him as a respected actor in the UK.

Following his success in "Star Trek: The Next Generation," Stewart continued to make notable contributions to film and television. He reprised his role as Captain Picard in the films "Star Trek: Generations" (1994), "Star Trek: First Contact" (1996), "Star Trek: Insurrection" (1998), and "Star Trek: Nemesis" (2002). In recent years, Stewart returned to the role of Picard in the television series "Star Trek: Picard" (2020-present), which explores the character's later life.

In addition to his work in the Star Trek franchise, Patrick Stewart has appeared in a wide range of films and television shows. Some of his notable film roles include Professor Charles Xavier in the "X-Men" series, Captain Ahab in "Moby Dick," and numerous other character-driven roles in both dramas and comedies.

Beyond his acting career, Stewart is known for his philanthropic efforts and advocacy work. He has been a strong advocate for various causes, including domestic violence, human rights, and animal rights. In 2010, he was knighted by Queen Elizabeth II for his services to drama.

Patrick Stewart's talent, versatility, and commitment to his craft have made him one of the most respected and beloved actors in the industry. His contributions to film, television, and theater have left a lasting impact, and his portrayal of Captain Jean-Luc Picard has become an iconic part of popular culture.

In addition to his acting career, Patrick Stewart has also ventured into directing. He made his directorial debut with the 1997 film "A Christmas Carol," in which he also starred as Ebenezer Scrooge. His directorial work extends to the theater as well, having directed several plays, including productions of Shakespeare's works.

Stewart's talents extend beyond the stage and screen. He is known for his distinctive voice, which has led to numerous voice acting roles. One of his most notable voice performances is as the character of Professor X in various animated adaptations of the X-Men franchise. His rich, commanding voice has also been utilized in documentaries, commercials, and even audiobooks.

In recent years, Stewart has continued to take on diverse and challenging roles, showcasing his range as an actor. He starred in the critically acclaimed television series "Blunt Talk" (2015-2016), where he portrayed a British news anchor struggling with personal and professional challenges. He also took on the role of Bosley in the action-comedy film "Charlie's Angels" (2019), adding his own unique spin to the iconic character.

Beyond his on-screen work, Patrick Stewart remains a beloved figure and a respected voice in the entertainment industry. He has been recognized with numerous awards throughout his career, including Golden Globe Awards, Screen Actors Guild Awards, and Emmy nominations. His contributions to the arts have earned him a place among the most esteemed actors of his generation.

Outside of his professional achievements, Stewart is known for his warm and approachable demeanor. He has been open about his own experiences with mental health challenges and has become an advocate for mental health awareness. He continues to use his platform to speak out on social issues, promote inclusivity, and support charitable causes.

Patrick Stewart's enduring talent, charisma, and dedication to his craft have made him a beloved figure for audiences worldwide. Whether on stage, in films, or in the realm of television, he continues to captivate audiences with his remarkable performances and leaves an indelible mark on the world of entertainment.

In addition to his impressive body of work, Patrick Stewart is also a respected figure in the academic world. He holds honorary degrees from several prestigious universities, including the University of Huddersfield, the University of East Anglia, and the University of Oxford. He has also been a visiting professor at the University of Connecticut, where he taught a class on Shakespearean acting.

Stewart's dedication to the arts extends beyond his own performances. He is a strong supporter of the theater community and has been involved in various initiatives to support emerging artists. He served as the Chancellor of the University of Huddersfield from 2004 to 2015, and during his tenure, he established a scholarship program to support students pursuing degrees in the arts.

In recent years, Stewart has also become an internet sensation, thanks to his hilarious and heartwarming social media presence. His tweets and Instagram posts, which often feature his adorable foster dog, have earned him a legion of fans online. He has also participated in various online challenges and trends, showcasing his fun-loving personality and endearing himself to audiences of all ages.

As he continues to take on new projects and challenges, Patrick Stewart remains a beloved figure in the entertainment industry and beyond. His impressive career, commitment to the arts, and charitable work have earned him the admiration and respect of fans worldwide. Whether on stage, screen, or social media, he continues to captivate audiences with his talent, charm, and infectious spirit.

In recent years, Patrick Stewart has embarked on new and exciting ventures, expanding his already impressive repertoire. In 2017, he starred in the critically acclaimed film "Logan," reprising his role as Professor Charles Xavier. The film received widespread praise for its gritty and emotional take on the superhero genre, and Stewart's nuanced performance was lauded as one of the highlights.

Stewart also surprised audiences by taking on a comedic role in the hit animated series "American Dad!" In the show, he provides the voice for the character Avery Bullock, the director of the CIA. His portrayal of Bullock showcases his versatility as an actor and his ability to tackle different genres with equal skill.

In 2020, Stewart returned to the Star Trek universe in the highly anticipated series "Star Trek: Picard." The show picks up years after the events of "Star Trek: The Next Generation" and follows the later adventures of Captain Jean-Luc Picard. Stewart's reprisal of the beloved character was met with great excitement from fans, and his performance once again captivated audiences with its depth and gravitas.

Aside from his acting work, Patrick Stewart remains committed to using his platform for social and political causes. He has been an outspoken advocate for LGBTQ+ rights and has been actively involved in campaigns to promote equality and fight against discrimination. His passionate stance on these issues has made him an influential figure and an inspiration to many.

In recognition of his contributions to the entertainment industry and his humanitarian efforts, Patrick Stewart has received numerous accolades and honors throughout his career. In addition to his knighthood, he has been awarded the Screen Actors Guild Life Achievement Award, the Empire Icon Award, and the Olivier Special Award, among others.

As he continues to delight audiences with his performances and champion important causes, Patrick Stewart remains an icon in the world of acting. His enduring talent, passion for the arts, and commitment to making a positive impact have solidified his status as a beloved figure both on and off the screen.

In 2020, during the COVID-19 pandemic, Patrick Stewart took on a new project that delighted fans and provided comfort during a challenging time. He began reading and sharing daily sonnets by William Shakespeare on social media platforms, under the hashtag #ASonnetADay. The series, which started as a way to uplift and entertain, quickly gained popularity and became a source of inspiration for many.

Stewart's love for Shakespeare has been evident throughout his career, and his sonnet readings showcased his deep connection to the playwright's works. His expressive voice and captivating delivery brought the timeless verses to life, allowing audiences to appreciate the beauty and power of Shakespeare's words from the comfort of their homes.

In addition to his sonnet readings, Stewart has continued to explore new avenues in his acting career. He starred in the science fiction thriller "Reminiscence" (2021) alongside Hugh Jackman, and he is set to appear in the highly anticipated film "Dune" (2023), based on the novel by Frank Herbert. These projects demonstrate Stewart's ability to adapt to different genres and collaborate with esteemed filmmakers.

Outside of his acting endeavors, Patrick Stewart remains an active supporter of various charitable organizations. He has been involved with organizations such as Amnesty International, the International Rescue Committee, and Refuge, all of which work to promote human rights and provide support to vulnerable communities. Stewart's dedication to these causes reflects his commitment to using his platform and influence for the betterment of society.

As a beloved figure in the entertainment industry, Patrick Stewart's impact extends far beyond his roles on stage and screen. His talent, versatility, and humanitarian efforts have earned him the admiration and respect of both his peers and audiences worldwide. Whether he is bringing iconic characters to life, lending his voice to important causes, or simply sharing his passion for literature, Patrick Stewart continues to captivate and inspire audiences with his remarkable presence.

In addition to his work in film, television, and theater, Patrick Stewart has also made significant contributions as a narrator and voice actor. His distinctive voice has been featured in various documentaries, commercials, and audiobooks. One notable project is his narration of the audiobook version of Charles Dickens' "A Christmas Carol," a fitting choice considering his past portrayal of Ebenezer Scrooge on stage.

Stewart's talent and contributions to the arts have not gone unnoticed. He has received numerous awards and honors throughout his career, including several Laurence Olivier Awards, a Tony Award, and a Critics' Choice Television Award. His impact on popular culture is also evident in his inclusion as a wax figure in Madame Tussauds museums in both London and New York City.

Outside of his professional achievements, Patrick Stewart has remained dedicated to his personal life as well. He has been an advocate for family and a strong supporter of his children. He has spoken openly about his own experiences with domestic violence and has used his platform to raise awareness about the issue.

In recent years, Stewart has continued to push boundaries and challenge himself creatively. He starred in the acclaimed television series "Star Trek: Picard," reprising his role as Jean-Luc Picard and exploring the character's later years. The show not only delighted fans of the Star Trek franchise but also introduced the beloved captain to a new generation of viewers.

Looking forward, it is clear that Patrick Stewart's influence and contributions to the entertainment industry will continue to endure. His passion for acting, his commitment to social causes, and his unwavering dedication to his craft have solidified his status as a true icon. Whether through his captivating performances, his philanthropy, or his engaging presence, Stewart continues to inspire and captivate audiences around the world.

Despite his illustrious career and many accomplishments, Patrick Stewart remains humble and grounded. He is known for his kindness and generosity towards fans, often taking time to interact with them at conventions and events. His genuine appreciation for his supporters has earned him a devoted and loyal fan base.

Stewart's impact goes beyond the realm of entertainment. His advocacy work extends to issues such as combatting domestic violence, supporting refugees and immigrants, and promoting equality and social justice. He has used his platform to speak out against injustices and to raise awareness about important causes. Stewart's activism has made a tangible difference and has inspired many others to use their voices for positive change.

In recognition of his outstanding contributions to the arts and his philanthropic efforts, Patrick Stewart was appointed an Officer of the Order of the British Empire (OBE) in 2001 and was later promoted to a Knight Bachelor in 2010. These honors further highlight his significant impact and his dedication to both his craft and society at large.

As time goes on, Patrick Stewart continues to captivate audiences with his performances, his unwavering passion for his craft, and his unwavering dedication to making a difference. Whether he's on stage, on screen, or using his voice for social change, Stewart remains an iconic figure whose talent and influence transcend generations. His legacy is one of exceptional talent, integrity, and a commitment to using his platform to better the world around him.

Stewart has been a vocal advocate for human rights, particularly in relation to domestic violence. He has spoken openly about his own experiences growing up in a household affected by domestic violence and has used his platform to raise awareness and support organizations working to combat this issue. His courage in sharing his personal story has helped shed light on a pervasive problem and has inspired many to seek help and speak out.

Furthermore, Stewart has been actively involved in organizations supporting refugees and immigrants. He has worked closely with the International Rescue Committee, an organization that provides assistance to displaced individuals around the world. Through his involvement, Stewart has sought to amplify the voices of those affected by displacement and to advocate for their rights and well-being.

Stewart's commitment to equality and social justice is evident in his advocacy for LGBTQ+ rights. He has been a vocal supporter of LGBTQ+ rights and has actively campaigned for marriage equality. Stewart has used his influence to foster inclusivity and acceptance, working to create a more equitable society for all.

In recognition of his significant contributions, Stewart has received several awards and honors for his activism, including the Amnesty International Award for Human Rights Advocacy. His dedication to using his platform to effect positive change showcases his integrity and the genuine care he has for making a difference in the world.

Patrick Stewart's impact extends far beyond his acting career. Through his advocacy, philanthropy, and activism, he has demonstrated a profound commitment to social causes and has inspired others to join him in creating a more compassionate and equitable society. His contributions to the arts and his humanitarian efforts have solidified his status as a respected and beloved figure, both on and off the screen.

In addition to his advocacy work, Patrick Stewart has also made significant contributions to the arts and education. He has been a staunch supporter of theater and has worked to promote the importance of arts education in schools. Stewart has participated in initiatives and programs aimed at nurturing young talent and providing opportunities for aspiring actors and artists.

Stewart's dedication to the theater extends to his own involvement in various productions. He has continued to take on challenging roles in both classic and contemporary plays. His stage performances have been met with critical acclaim, further solidifying his reputation as a consummate actor with a deep understanding of the craft.

Furthermore, Patrick Stewart's influence extends to his role as a mentor and inspiration for aspiring actors. He has shared his knowledge and experience through teaching and conducting acting workshops. By passing on his wisdom and skills to the next generation, Stewart has played a vital role in shaping the future of the performing arts.

Outside of his professional pursuits, Stewart is known for his down-to-earth nature and approachability. Despite his fame, he has remained humble and has always been appreciative of his fans. He has been known to take time to interact with fans, sign autographs, and participate in fan conventions, making a genuine connection with those who admire his work.

Patrick Stewart's impact on the entertainment industry, advocacy work, and contributions to the arts and education are a testament to his multifaceted talent and unwavering dedication. His legacy goes beyond his remarkable performances and encompasses his commitment to using his platform for positive change. Stewart's influence continues to inspire generations of actors, artists, and individuals striving to make a difference in the world.

# Acting career
## Early acting career (1959–1987)

Patrick Stewart's early acting career spanned from 1959 to 1987 and laid the foundation for his subsequent success in the entertainment industry. Here's a glimpse into this period:

Stewart began his acting journey in the late 1950s, initially working in repertory theater and honing his skills in various stage productions. He gained experience in both classical and contemporary plays, performing with renowned theater companies such as the Bristol Old Vic and the Royal Shakespeare Company (RSC). During this time, he established himself as a versatile and talented actor, capable of portraying a wide range of characters.

In 1966, Stewart made his debut with the Royal Shakespeare Company in a production of "Coriolanus." This marked the beginning of his longstanding association with the RSC, where he would go on to deliver memorable performances in numerous Shakespearean plays. He showcased his talent and versatility through roles like Shylock in "The Merchant of Venice," Macbeth in "Macbeth," and Prospero in "The Tempest."

Stewart's commitment to the theater continued throughout the 1970s and 1980s. He received critical acclaim for his performances in plays such as "Antony and Cleopatra," "Julius Caesar," and "Othello." His mastery of Shakespearean language and his ability to bring depth and complexity to his characters earned him recognition as one of the finest stage actors of his generation.

During this period, Stewart also made appearances in various television productions, including dramas and adaptations of literary works. Notably, he played the lead role of Sejanus in the BBC miniseries "I, Claudius" (1976) and portrayed the character Karla in the television adaptation of John le Carré's "Tinker Tailor Soldier Spy" (1979).

In 1987, Patrick Stewart's career took a significant turn with his casting as Captain Jean-Luc Picard in the television series "Star Trek: The Next Generation." The role brought him international recognition and catapulted him into the mainstream. Stewart's portrayal of Picard, a wise and principled leader, resonated with audiences and solidified his place as a beloved actor in the science fiction genre.

The early years of Patrick Stewart's acting career laid the groundwork for his later achievements. His dedication to the stage, his mastery of Shakespeare, and his early television appearances showcased his talent and versatility. These formative years paved the way for the iconic roles and acclaimed performances that would follow in the years to come.

# Film and TV career (1987–present)
## Star Trek: The Next Generation

Patrick Stewart's film and TV career took a significant turn in 1987 when he was cast as Captain Jean-Luc Picard in the television series "Star Trek: The Next Generation." The show, which ran for seven seasons until 1994, brought Stewart widespread recognition and made him an iconic figure in the science fiction genre.

As Captain Picard, Stewart portrayed a thoughtful and diplomatic leader of the starship USS Enterprise-D. His performance resonated with audiences, showcasing his ability to bring depth and complexity to the character. Stewart's portrayal of Picard was distinguished by his commanding presence, nuanced acting, and a memorable voice that captivated viewers.

"Star Trek: The Next Generation" became a critical and commercial success, earning a devoted fan base and expanding the "Star Trek" franchise. The show explored complex moral and philosophical themes while entertaining audiences with its compelling storytelling. Stewart's performance as Picard earned him widespread acclaim and several award nominations, solidifying his place as a pop culture icon.

Following the end of "Star Trek: The Next Generation," Stewart reprised the role of Captain Picard in several feature films, including "Star Trek: Generations" (1994), "Star Trek: First Contact" (1996), "Star Trek: Insurrection" (1998), and "Star Trek: Nemesis" (2002). These films allowed him to further delve into the character and expand upon Picard's journey.

Beyond the "Star Trek" franchise, Stewart has been involved in numerous film and television projects. Notably, he portrayed Professor Charles Xavier, the leader of the X-Men, in the highly successful "X-Men" film series. His portrayal of the wise and telepathic mutant showcased his versatility as an actor and further endeared him to audiences worldwide.

Stewart's filmography also includes diverse roles in films such as "Dune" (1984), "Jeffrey" (1995), "The Match" (1999), "Logan" (2017), and "Green Room" (2015). His ability to tackle both dramatic and comedic roles has earned him praise and recognition from critics and audiences alike.

In recent years, Stewart has returned to the "Star Trek" universe with the series "Star Trek: Picard" (2020-present). The show follows an older Jean-Luc Picard as he embarks on new adventures and faces the challenges of a changed galaxy. Stewart's reprisal of the beloved character has been met with enthusiasm and has reignited the excitement of "Star Trek" fans.

Throughout his film and TV career, Patrick Stewart has demonstrated his immense talent, versatility, and ability to bring compelling characters to life. His portrayal of Captain Picard and other memorable roles has solidified his status as a respected and beloved actor, both within the science fiction genre and beyond.

# Documentaries

Patrick Stewart has lent his distinctive voice and presence to various documentaries, adding his talents to bring depth and narration to these projects. Here are some notable documentaries in which he has been involved:

"The Secret Policeman's Other Ball" (1982): Stewart hosted this documentary film that captured the highlights of the live comedy and music event held in support of Amnesty International. The event featured performances by renowned comedians and musicians, and Stewart's hosting added a touch of elegance and gravitas to the proceedings.

"The Making of Star Wars: The Empire Strikes Back" (1980): Stewart narrated this behind-the-scenes documentary that explored the production of the iconic film. His authoritative voice guided viewers through the intricate process of bringing the Star Wars universe to life, providing fascinating insights into the filmmaking techniques used in the second installment of the original trilogy.

"Circus" (2010): In this documentary series, Stewart served as the narrator, guiding viewers through the world of the traveling circus. The series delved into the lives of performers, the challenges they faced, and the rich history and traditions of the circus. Stewart's narration added a layer of storytelling and gravitas to the captivating visuals.

"Animal Farm: A Fairy Story" (2014): Stewart provided the narration for this documentary adaptation of George Orwell's classic novel "Animal Farm." His voice brought the characters and themes of the allegorical story to life, adding depth and emotional resonance to the powerful tale of political corruption and social injustice.

"The Jazz Ambassadors" (2018): In this documentary, Stewart lent his voice to narrate the story of American jazz musicians who were sent as cultural ambassadors during the Cold War. The film explores the role of jazz in diplomacy and cultural exchange, highlighting the impact these musicians had in shaping perceptions and breaking down barriers.

# Other film and television

Film:

"Excalibur" (1981): Stewart played the role of King Leondegrance in this epic fantasy film directed by John Boorman, which depicted the Arthurian legend.

"L.A. Story" (1991): Stewart had a memorable cameo as a witty British butler in this romantic comedy film written by and starring Steve Martin.

"Safe House" (1998): Stewart portrayed a mysterious and enigmatic character named Mace Sowell in this thriller film directed by Eric Steven Stahl.

"Jeffrey" (1995): Stewart appeared as Sterling, a wise and empathetic character, in this romantic comedy-drama film based on a play by Paul Rudnick.

"X-Men" Film Series (2000-2017): Stewart portrayed the telepathic mutant Professor Charles Xavier in the popular superhero franchise, appearing in multiple films including "X-Men" (2000), "X2: X-Men United" (2003), "X-Men: The Last Stand" (2006), and "Logan" (2017).

Television:

"I, Claudius" (1976): Stewart played the role of Lucius Aelius Sejanus, a powerful Roman military officer, in this acclaimed BBC miniseries based on the Roman history novels by Robert Graves.

"Tinker Tailor Soldier Spy" (1979): Stewart portrayed the character Karla, a high-ranking Soviet spy, in the television adaptation of John le Carré's famous spy novel.

"Blunt Talk" (2015-2016): Stewart starred as Walter Blunt, a British news anchor trying to conquer the American media landscape, in this satirical comedy series created by Jonathan Ames.

"American Dad!" (2005-present): Stewart has lent his voice to the animated sitcom, providing the voice for Avery Bullock, the director of the Central Intelligence Agency (CIA).

These are just a few examples of Patrick Stewart's extensive film and television credits. His versatile performances and ability to embody a range of characters have allowed him to make an indelible mark across various genres and mediums throughout his career.

# Theatre (1990–present)

Patrick Stewart's involvement in theatre has remained a significant part of his career from 1990 to the present. Here are some notable highlights of his theatrical work during this period:

"A Christmas Carol" (1991): Stewart embarked on a one-man production of Charles Dickens' classic holiday tale, captivating audiences with his solo performance. The production received critical acclaim and became a beloved tradition, with Stewart reprising the role in subsequent years.

"The Tempest" (1995): Stewart took on the iconic role of Prospero in Shakespeare's "The Tempest" for a Royal Shakespeare Company production. His portrayal showcased his mastery of the Bard's language and his ability to bring depth and complexity to the character.

"Hamlet" (2008): Stewart played the role of Claudius, the treacherous uncle of the title character, in a critically acclaimed production of Shakespeare's "Hamlet" directed by Rupert Goold. His performance garnered praise for its nuanced portrayal of the conflicted and manipulative character.

"Waiting for Godot" (2009): Stewart teamed up with his close friend and fellow actor Ian McKellen for a production of Samuel Beckett's absurdist play, "Waiting for Godot." The duo's chemistry and performances as Vladimir and Estragon, respectively, received acclaim and drew audiences from around the world.

"No Man's Land" (2016): Stewart reunited with Ian McKellen once again for a revival of Harold Pinter's play, "No Man's Land." The production, directed by Sean Mathias, showcased the dynamic between the two actors in a gripping exploration of power, memory, and identity.

"The Ride Down Mount Morgan" (2020): Stewart starred in a revival of Arthur Miller's play, "The Ride Down Mount Morgan," in London's West End. His performance as Lyman Felt, a man leading a double life, earned critical acclaim for its complexity and emotional depth.

Throughout his career, Patrick Stewart has continued to prioritize his work in the theatre, returning to the stage to challenge himself with a variety of roles. His command of the stage, nuanced performances, and deep understanding of the texts have solidified his reputation as a masterful stage actor. Stewart's commitment to the theatrical arts has allowed him to engage with classical and contemporary works, captivating audiences with his craft and leaving a lasting impact on the world of theatre.

# Voice work

Patrick Stewart has also made significant contributions to the world of voice work, lending his distinct voice to various projects. His deep, resonant voice and commanding presence have made him a sought-after voice actor. Here are some notable examples of his voice work:

"The Iron Giant" (1999): Stewart provided the voice for the character of Kent Mansley, a government agent, in this critically acclaimed animated film. His voice brought depth and intensity to the character, adding to the film's emotional impact.

"Chicken Little" (2005): Stewart voiced the character of Mr. Woolensworth, a sheep and the father of the film's protagonist. His voice work contributed to the humor and charm of the animated comedy.

"The Prince of Egypt" (1998): Stewart provided the voice for Pharaoh Seti I in this animated biblical epic. His commanding voice lent gravitas to the character, embodying the regal and authoritative nature of the Pharaoh.

"American Dad!" (2005-present): Stewart has been a regular cast member on this animated sitcom, lending his voice to the character of Avery Bullock, the director of the CIA. His voice work adds humor and depth to the character, making him one of the show's most memorable figures.

"The Elder Scrolls IV: Oblivion" (2006): Stewart voiced the character of Emperor Uriel Septim VII in this critically acclaimed video game. His performance brought an air of authority and wisdom to the character, enhancing the immersive experience of the game.

"The Nightmare Before Christmas" (1993): While Stewart did not provide a voice for this stop-motion animated film, he served as the narrator, lending his voice to the opening and closing narration. His rich and captivating voice set the tone for the fantastical world of the film.

These are just a few examples of Patrick Stewart's voice work. His distinctive voice and expressive delivery have made him a highly sought-after voice actor, adding depth and character to various animated films, TV shows, and video games. His contributions to the realm of voice acting have further showcased his versatility and talent as a performer.

# Awards and honours

Patrick Stewart's remarkable career has been recognized with numerous awards and honors throughout the years. Here are some notable accolades he has received:

Tony Awards: Stewart has been nominated for and won several Tony Awards, which honor achievements in Broadway theater. He received the following:

1991: Tony Award for Best Actor in a Play for his performance in "A Christmas Carol."
2008: Special Tony Award for Lifetime Achievement in the Theatre, recognizing his outstanding contributions to the stage.
Screen Actors Guild Awards: Stewart has been honored with multiple Screen Actors Guild (SAG) Awards for his work in television and film. Notable wins include:

1995: SAG Award for Outstanding Performance by an Ensemble in a Drama Series for "Star Trek: The Next Generation."
1997: SAG Award for Outstanding Performance by a Cast in a Motion Picture for his role in "The Lion in Winter."
Primetime Emmy Awards: Stewart has been nominated for Primetime Emmy Awards for his performances in various television projects, including:

1993: Primetime Emmy Award nomination for Outstanding Lead Actor in a Drama Series for "Star Trek: The Next Generation."
2017: Primetime Emmy Award nomination for Outstanding Supporting Actor in a Limited Series or Movie for "No Man's Land."
Laurence Olivier Awards: Stewart has been recognized by the prestigious Laurence Olivier Awards, which celebrate excellence in British theatre. Notable nominations include:

1991: Laurence Olivier Award nomination for Best Actor for his portrayal of Prospero in "The Tempest."
2003: Laurence Olivier Award nomination for Best Actor for his role in "The Master Builder."
Honorary Awards: In addition to specific awards for his performances, Stewart has received various honorary awards for his contributions to the entertainment industry, including:

2010: Knight Bachelor: Stewart was knighted by Queen Elizabeth II in recognition of his services to drama.
2017: Critics' Choice Television Awards Lifetime Achievement Award: He was honored for his exceptional contributions to television.

# Charity work and activism

Patrick Stewart has been actively involved in various charitable endeavors and has used his platform to advocate for important causes. Here are some examples of his charity work and activism:

Combat Stress: Stewart has been a prominent supporter of Combat Stress, a charity that provides mental health support to veterans. He has served as a patron and actively raised awareness and funds for the organization.

Amnesty International: Stewart has been a long-standing supporter of Amnesty International, an organization dedicated to human rights advocacy. He has participated in various events and campaigns to raise awareness about human rights violations around the world.

Refuge: Stewart has been a vocal advocate for Refuge, a charity that supports victims of domestic violence. He has campaigned to raise awareness of the issue and has spoken out against domestic violence in interviews and public appearances.

Make-A-Wish Foundation: Stewart has been involved with the Make-A-Wish Foundation, which grants the wishes of children with life-threatening illnesses. He has granted wishes and has supported fundraising efforts for the organization.

Stonewall: Stewart has been an ally and supporter of the LGBTQ+ community. He has actively worked with Stonewall, a charity that promotes LGBTQ+ rights and equality, and has been involved in campaigns to raise awareness and combat discrimination.

Animal Rights: Stewart has been an advocate for animal rights and has supported organizations such as PETA (People for the Ethical Treatment of Animals). He has spoken out against animal cruelty and has promoted the adoption of rescue animals.

In addition to his involvement with specific charities, Stewart has used his public platform to speak out on various social and political issues. He has been a vocal critic of domestic violence, discrimination, and social injustice, using his voice to raise awareness and promote positive change.

Patrick Stewart's charitable work and activism demonstrate his commitment to making a difference in the lives of others and his dedication to fighting for a more just and equitable world. His involvement in these causes has not only raised awareness but has also inspired others to get involved and support important social issues.

Personal life

ChatGPT

Patrick Stewart's personal life encompasses his relationships, interests, and experiences outside of his professional career. Here are some details about his personal life:

Marriages and Family: Stewart has been married three times. His first marriage was to Sheila Falconer, an actress, in 1966. They have two children together, Daniel and Sophia. The couple divorced in 1990. Stewart's second marriage was to television producer Wendy Neuss, whom he married in 2000 and divorced in 2003. In 2013, he married jazz singer Sunny Ozell, and they have been together since.

Hobbies and Interests: Outside of his work, Stewart has various hobbies and interests. He is an avid supporter of his favorite football team, Huddersfield Town AFC. He also enjoys playing the guitar and has occasionally performed music in public, including jazz and blues. Additionally, he is a lover of literature and poetry, and he often shares his favorite works with his fans.

Advocacy and Philanthropy: As mentioned earlier, Stewart is involved in various charitable causes and activism. He has used his platform to advocate for issues such as mental health, human rights, domestic violence, and animal rights. He actively participates in fundraising events and supports organizations that work towards positive social change.

Friendship with Ian McKellen: Stewart and fellow actor Ian McKellen have a close friendship that has spanned several decades. They have worked together on numerous projects, including the "X-Men" film series and various stage productions. Their camaraderie and shared sense of humor are often evident in their public appearances and social media posts.

Honors and Recognition: In addition to the professional awards mentioned earlier, Patrick Stewart has received several honors and recognition for his contributions to the arts. In 2010, he was awarded a knighthood by Queen Elizabeth II for his services to drama. This title allows him to be addressed as "Sir Patrick Stewart."

# Audiobooks

Patrick Stewart has lent his distinctive voice and storytelling abilities to several audiobook projects, bringing classic literature and popular works to life. Here are some notable audiobooks that he has narrated:

"A Christmas Carol" by Charles Dickens: Stewart's connection to this beloved holiday story extends beyond his stage performances. He has recorded a captivating audiobook version of "A Christmas Carol," in which his expressive narration enhances the timeless tale.

"The War of the Worlds" by H.G. Wells: Stewart's commanding voice is a perfect fit for this science fiction classic. His narration adds intensity and suspense to the thrilling story of an alien invasion.

"The Handmaid's Tale" by Margaret Atwood: Stewart lends his voice to the audiobook version of this dystopian novel, providing a haunting and chilling rendition that captures the essence of the story's dark themes.

"The Once and Future King" by T.H. White: Stewart's narration brings to life the Arthurian legend in this classic fantasy novel. His rich and evocative voice transports listeners to the magical world of Camelot.

"Treasure Island" by Robert Louis Stevenson: Stewart's expressive storytelling skills shine in this adventure tale of pirates and buried treasure. His dynamic narration captivates listeners and immerses them in the thrilling journey.

"Great Expectations" by Charles Dickens: Stewart's narration of this iconic Dickens novel captures the depth and complexity of the characters, drawing listeners into the world of Pip and his journey of self-discovery.

These are just a few examples of the audiobooks that Patrick Stewart has narrated. His captivating voice, nuanced delivery, and ability to bring characters to life make his audiobook performances highly engaging and enjoyable. Whether it's a classic novel or a contemporary work, his narrations add an extra layer of immersion and enjoyment to the listening experience.

Printed in Great Britain
by Amazon